The Navy in Action

Ann Graham Gaines
AR B.L.: 9.4
Points: 3.0   UG

THE NAVY IN ACTION

Titles in *U.S. Military Branches and Careers*

The Air Force in Action
ISBN 0-7660-1636-6

The Army in Action
ISBN 0-7660-1635-8

The Coast Guard in Action
ISBN 0-7660-1634-X

The Marine Corps in Action
ISBN 0-7660-1637-4

The Navy in Action
ISBN 0-7660-1633-1

U.S. Military Branches and Careers

THE NAVY IN ACTION

Ann Graham Gaines

Enslow Publishers, Inc.

40 Industrial Road   PO Box 38
Box 398   Aldershot
Berkeley Heights, NJ 07922   Hants GU12 6BP
USA   UK

http://www.enslow.com

Library of Congress Cataloging-in-Publication Data
Gaines, Ann.
    The Navy in action / Ann Graham Gaines.
       p. cm. — (U.S. military branches and careers)
    Includes bibliographical references (p.   ) and index.
    ISBN 0-7660-1633-1
    United States. Navy—Vocational guidance—Juvenile literature.
    [1. United States. Navy. 2. United States. Navy—Vocational guidance.
    3. Vocational guidance.] I.Titles II. Series.
    VB259 .G35 2001
    359'.00973—dc21

                                          00-010154

Printed in the United States of America

10 9 8 7 6 5 4 3

To Our Readers: We have done our best to make sure all Internet addresses in
this book were active and appropriate when we went to press. However, the
author and the publisher have no control over and assume no liability for the
material available on those Internet sites or on other Web sites they may link to.
Any comments or suggestions can be sent by e-mail to comments@enslow.com or
to the address on the back cover.

Illustration Credits: Corel Corp., pp. 78–79, 103; Library of Congress,
pp. 42, 98; National Archives, pp. 6–7, 14–15, 16, 19, 20, 22, 24, 25,
30–31, 32, 36, 40, 52, 54, 70–71, 84, 90, 92; United States Department
of Defense, pp. 11, 35, 45, 46, 48, 51, 57, 58, 61, 72, 74, 85, 86, 89,
91, 94, 96, 106, 107, 108, 110, 111, 112; United States Navy, p. 62;
Jennifer Grob, p. 81.

Cover Illustration: U.S. Department of Defense.

Contents

⭐1 "We Have Met the Enemy
and They Are Ours" 6

⭐2 History of the United
States Navy 13

⭐3 Joining the Navy 39

⭐4 Structure of the United
States Navy 60

⭐5 Careers in the Navy...... 68

⭐6 Women and Minorities
in the Navy 83

⭐7 The Future 101

Weapons, Technology,
and Ships............... 105

Chapter Notes 115

Glossary 121

Further Reading.......... 124

Internet Addresses........ 125

Index.................. 126

"We Have Met the Enemy and They Are Ours"

When President James Madison declared war on Great Britain on June 18, 1812, the British Navy was the largest in the world. It had more than seven hundred ships and tens of thousands of experienced sailors. Few people thought the fledgling United States Navy—which had less than twenty ships—had any chance against this powerful force.

Leaders of both Great Britain and the United States believed that control of Lake Erie, one of the Great Lakes forming the boundary between British Canada and the United States, was vital to winning the war. In March 1813 an American naval officer, twenty-seven-year-old Oliver Hazard Perry, was sent to supervise the construction of a fleet and to seize control of Lake Erie. To do so would mean engaging the British, who already had ships there.

Perry oversaw the building of two man-of-war brigs, the USS *Lawrence*

Control of Lake Erie was vital to winning the War of 1812 for both the Americans and the British. This engraving depicts Master Commandant Oliver Hazard Perry (standing) at the Battle of Lake Erie in September, 1813.

and the USS *Niagara*, and four smaller armed schooners. Everything, other than local lumber—the ships' guns, ammunition, canvas, ropes—had to be hauled overland from Pittsburgh, one hundred miles inland, or sailed from Buffalo across a lake. Perry and his men could not have managed this amazing feat had they not possessed unflagging energy, courage, and nerve.

Only 490 men manned the American vessels, less than the usual required crew of 740. Perry filled the ships with any men he could find: Native Americans, frontiersmen, African Americans, and even a Russian who could not speak a word of English. One hundred of the crew members were militiamen from Kentucky and Pennsylvania. They would be stationed on the ships' masts and used as sharpshooters against the enemy.

The British ships already stationed on the lake faced a desperate situation. They had almost run out of food and supplies. The British commander, Lieutenant Robert Heriot Barclay, knew he had to fight or surrender.

At sunrise on September 10, 1813, the lookouts on the *Lawrence*, Perry's flagship, spied the enemy in the distance. Perry led his small fleet to meet the oncoming British force. When the *Lawrence* came within range, the British fired their cannons. The first British cannonballs fell short of the American ship, but the second volley struck home. Although Perry signaled for his other ships to follow the *Lawrence*, for some unexplained reason, they remained behind, their crews watching the battle. Alone, Perry and his crew endured volley after volley. Finally, the *Lawrence* glided close enough to the enemy to use her heavier but shorter range guns. The three biggest British ships, the HMS *Detroit*, the HMS *Queen Charlotte*, and the HMS *General Hunter*, faced the lone American vessel.

For two hours the enemies traded volleys. Enemy sharpshooters in the riggings of the ships ambushed sailors as they brought new balls and powder to the cannons or carried the wounded below decks. During the battle, all the captains and first officers on the three British ships were either killed or wounded. Lieutenant Barclay was wounded four times before he allowed his men to carry him below deck. Through it all, Perry remained on the main deck of the *Lawrence*, untouched by enemy fire.

As the battle raged, the men on the other American ships continued to watch from out of harm's way. By one-thirty the *Lawrence*'s masts, sails, and rigging were completely destroyed. Eighty-three of the 110 men aboard had either been killed or lay wounded. It seemed hopeless, yet Perry was not ready to surrender.

He had four seamen row him to the USS *Niagara*, a half mile away. Sailors on the damaged British ships saw what Perry was doing and tried to hit his rowboat, but they failed. When Perry reached the *Niagara*, he ordered the captain into the waiting rowboat and sent him to bring up the other American vessels waiting behind. Then Perry sailed the *Niagara* to join the battle immediately.

Perry returned to the battle with a fresh ship, fresh crew, and fresh cannonades. He thrust the *Niagara* in between the British ships, which were nearly as badly off as the *Lawrence*. As the *Queen Charlotte* and the *Detroit* tried to turn to use their undamaged starboard guns on the American ship, their broken masts and spars became entangled. With the senior officers dead or wounded, the British junior officers were not equal to the situation that faced them. All twenty cannons of the *Niagara* fired at the severely damaged British ships. What had not been destroyed and bloodied by the *Lawrence* was now the victim of the *Niagara*.

The *Detroit* fired a cannon, signaling her surrender, and the *Queen Charlotte* raised a white flag. It was over. Barclay had surrendered the British fleet. Perry understood the importance of his victory—never before had an entire British fleet surrendered to anyone, anywhere!

General William Henry Harrison, the commander of the American forces and a future president of the United States, waited ashore. Perry quickly penned him a note saying: "We have met the enemy and they are ours: Two Ships, two Brigs, one schooner & one Sloop. Yours, with great respect and esteem. O. H. Perry."[1]

Today's Navy

The United States Navy has come a long way since the days of its earliest heroes. Almost two hundred years have passed since the Battle of Lake Erie. Oliver Hazard Perry and his crew would be amazed and proud of the way their navy looks in the twenty-first century.

The navy is a huge and powerful force, an extremely important part of the defenses built up by the United States. Its vessels, which include aircraft

Today's navy is a huge and powerful force, with technologically equipped vessels like this destroyer, the USS *Ross*.

carriers, cruisers, destroyers, frigates, support ships, and submarines, are equipped with advanced technology. They patrol the world's oceans and are capable of offensive and defensive operations in every kind of environment, under, on, and above the surface of the seas.

In June 2000 the navy counted 315 ships and almost 370,000 active duty men and women to operate and maintain them.[2] Some of the more than four thousand aircraft, aboard ships and on land bases, offer support. The navy has largely replaced its guns with more deadly, accurate, and longer-range missiles. In space, satellites are capable of aiding the navy's weapons systems to pinpoint targets anywhere in the world. Sophisticated radar and sonar technologies make the navy's ships almost invulnerable to a surprise attack. It is a formidable navy.

When it counts, however, it is not the sophistication or number of weapons that win battles. Rather, it is the courage and devotion to duty like those sailors showed in the Battle of Lake Erie. Those who supervise the United States military know this. They make sure the primary business of the navy is not weapons but its men and women.

History of the United States Navy

In 1775 all of the British colonies in North America were located along the Atlantic Ocean. Most towns were also seaports. There were many products that the colonists needed for their homes and businesses that were not made in the colonies. To obtain them, the colonists had to trade with other countries around the world. All of this trade was conducted aboard ships, many of which were built in America and were manned mostly by American colonists. Altogether, more than 2,500 American merchant ships sailed around the world, trading in places as far away as China and India.

When the American Revolution broke out near Boston in the battles of Lexington and Concord in April 1775, American sailors quickly joined the conflict. They attacked whatever British ships they could find and captured a number of the enemy's vessels.

First Navy

The United States Navy officially came into being on October 13, 1775, when the Continental Congress in Philadelphia set aside the money to build two ships capable of capturing British merchant ships. By December 1775, Congress had approved the construction of thirteen more warships. At that time, the British Navy was the greatest in the world, with over five hundred warships.

John Paul Jones

One of the most famous naval heroes of the Revolutionary War was John Paul Jones. On September 23, 1779, off the east coast of England, the *Bonhomme Richard* and other American ships under the command of John Paul

When the British HMS *Serapis* sank the *Bonhomme Richard* in September, 1779, American naval hero John Paul Jones uttered his famous cry, "No, I have just begun to fight!" Jones boarded the *Serapis*, engaging in violent hand-to-hand combat that eventually led to an important American victory.

Jones engaged a large British merchant fleet protected by the HMS *Serapis*, a new and deadly British man-of-war.

Jones sailed his ship directly toward the *Serapis*, even though he was outgunned. When they were within range, each ship fired. Two of the cannons aboard the *Bonhomme Richard* exploded, killing their crews

and blowing a hole in the main deck of the ship. One by one, the guns of the *Bonhomme Richard* fell silent as British cannonballs destroyed the hull and killed the gun crews inside. Captain Jones had but one choice left: to come alongside the *Serapis*, board her, and win the fight in hand-to-hand combat. As the *Bonhomme Richard* came alongside, the *Serapis* fired one final broadside and the gun deck of the American ship came apart. A voice from the *Serapis* asked if the Americans were ready to surrender. Captain Jones replied loudly, "No, I have just begun to fight!"[1]

American marines boarded the *Serapis* and intense and deadly fighting continued for three hours. Slowly, the tide turned to favor the Americans. With both

Lieutenant Stephen Decatur and Midshipman Thomas Mcdonough boarding an enemy gun boat during attack on Tripoli by the squadron under Commodore Preble on August 3, 1804.

ships littered with the dead and dying, the British captain surrendered. The *Bonhomme Richard* sank on the spot, and Jones took over the *Serapis* as his new flagship. It was a tremendous victory, and it established the reputation of the courage and skill of American sailors.

The Barbary Pirates

After the Revolutionary War, the rulers of several small countries along the African coast of the Mediterranean Sea, known as the Barbary Coast, made money by robbing the merchant ships that sailed through the nearby Straits of Gibraltar. The United States, like other countries such as Britain, had been paying the Barbary pirates not to attack their ships. When Congress refused to continue the payments in 1801, the pasha of Tripoli declared war on the United States. The United States sent squadrons of ships to fight the pirates in 1801 and 1802. However, the pirates, using small boats that could operate in

Edward Preble (1761–1807)

Edward Preble entered the Massachusetts State navy in 1780. With only fourteen men aboard the USS *Winthrop*, he captured the British ship HMS *Merriam* off the coast of Maine. In 1803 he was appointed commander of the third squadron and sent to the Mediterranean Sea in the war with Tripoli (1801 1805). Aboard the USS *Constitution*, Preble conducted daring raids against the pirates of Tripoli in August and September 1804 that helped to secure foreign recognition of American ships abroad.

shallow water, simply ran away from the larger American ships and hid in the shallow harbors, protected by their guns on shore.

In 1803, Captain Edward Preble on the USS *Constitution* brought along several small ships that could sail directly into the Barbary Coast's shallow harbors. In October a large American warship, the USS *Philadelphia*, ran aground outside of Tripoli harbor. The captain, William Bainbridge, was forced to surrender his ship. But Captain Preble created a daring plan to destroy the *Philadelphia* before the pirates could use it against other American ships.

He sent Lieutenant Stephen Decatur, Jr., along with nine sailors and a pilot, all disguised, into the harbor of Tripoli in a small pirate boat they had captured. Below decks were seventy-five other American sailors and a large store of explosives. As soon as the two ships were close, the disguised American sailors scrambled aboard the *Philadelphia* and began to fight for control of the ship, killing twenty pirates in a few minutes. Decatur ordered the sailors waiting below decks to carry the explosives onto the *Philadelphia* and set them off. Within twenty minutes, the *Philadelphia* was engulfed in flames, and the Americans quickly reboarded their small boat and escaped. The pasha of Tripoli was so furious when he found out that he demanded that the Americans pay him for the *Philadelphia*. Captain Preble laughed when he heard that.[2]

Raphael Semmes
(1809–1877)

In 1826, President John Quincy Adams appointed Semmes a midshipman in the navy. He served in the Mediterranean Sea, the South Atlantic Ocean, and along the coast of Mexico during the Mexican War (1846 1848). When the Civil War (1861 1865) broke out, Semmes commanded the first Confederate commerce raider, the CSS *Sumter*, and captured eighteen ships. He was promoted and given command of the raider CSS *Alabama*, which sailed 75,000 miles around the world capturing sixty-four more prize ships. On June 19, 1864, the *Alabama* was sunk by the Union ship USS *Kearsarge* off the coast of Cherbourg, France, in a battle watched by thousands of spectators along the French cliffs. Shown are the officers of the *Kearsarge* on deck in 1864.

Civil War and the Ironclads

When the Civil War began in 1861, the Confederacy quickly found out that it could not supply its forces with the guns, gunpowder, medicines, and hundreds of other goods that its army needed. The Union navy had set up a blockade of southern ports, which had a serious impact on the South's ability to get needed supplies and materials. Most of the efforts of the Confederate navy were attempts to defeat this blockade.

With its flat deck and a single revolving turret, people compared the *Monitor* to a "cheesebox on a raft." Though funny looking, this ironclad, commissioned on March 4, 1862, was an important innovation for the Union forces.

In May 1861, Stephen Mallory, the Confederate secretary of the navy, wrote his naval committee: "I regard the possession of an iron-armored ship as a matter of the first necessity." Mallory had the hull of a captured Union steamship, the USS *Merrimac*, covered with two coats of two-inch-thick iron plates placed at a sloping angle. Although the *Merrimac*, rechristened CSS *Virginia*, was not the first ironclad ship ever built, her design and construction were a process of trial and error. Many said that she would never float or steer or predicted she would flip upside down when launched. When completed, the *Virginia* looked like a long iron box with sides sloped up to make a wide roof of wood that left openings for light and air. Its sides showed ten cannons and it carried a 1,500-pound ram at the bow. Despite all the worry, it was launched without a problem and handled perfectly. Mallory later said, "You have no idea what I have suffered in mind since I commenced her; but I knew what I was about, and persevered."[3]

When the secretary of the Union navy, Gideon Welles, learned of the ironclad being constructed at Norfolk, Virginia, he signed contracts for three Union ironclads. One, the *Monitor*, was even more peculiar looking than the *Virginia*. Like the *Virginia*, the *Monitor* had a conventional hull. But above the waterline, the *Monitor* had a flat deck with a single revolving turret in the middle equipped with two cannons. Many people commented that the ship looked like a "cheesebox on a raft."[4] The *Monitor* was

George Dewey
(1837–1917)

George Dewey graduated from the Naval Academy in 1858. He served with distinction in the Union navy during the blockade of southern ports during the Civil War (1861 1865). During the 1870s and 1880s, he led a surveying expedition to the Gulf of California and was secretary of the Lighthouse Board in Washington, D.C. On May 1, 1898, when war was declared against Spain, Dewey led the American squadron into Manila Bay and destroyed the Spanish fleet there. During that summer, he arranged for the Spanish surrender of the Philippine Islands to the United States. In 1899 he was made an admiral of the navy. Shown is the Battle of Manila in 1898.

commissioned on March 4, 1862, and quickly towed to Chesapeake Bay. She arrived in the evening of March 8, just a few hours too late to stop the *Virginia* from attacking the Union fleet assembled there.

On March 8, 1862, at the mouth of the James River where it enters Chesapeake Bay, five Union ships were cruising to blockade the port. The *Virginia* attacked them each in turn. She badly damaged one of the heavily armed sailing frigates and rammed and sunk the sloop USS *Cumberland*. She attacked the other fifty-gun frigate, the USS *Congress*, forcing the ship to surrender. The fifth ship, the USS *Minnesota*, ran aground trying to flee the still-undamaged *Virginia*.

The next morning, the *Virginia* steamed back into Hampton Roads, Virginia, and headed for the grounded *Minnesota*. In her path was the *Monitor*. For hours the two ironclads fired cannonballs at each other at close range. After four hours neither ship was damaged enough to surrender. The first battle between ironclad ships ended as a draw. Never again would wooden-hulled ships be built as a nation's first line of defense.

The Submarine

Another effort on the part of the Confederacy to defeat the Union blockade was the so-called submarine CSS *David*. It operated with its stack and hatches above the surface of the water. Although it was not very successful, the Confederate navy continued to work on the development of the submarine. The most successful one, the CSS *Hunley*, was propelled by hand cranks and actually submerged, but it did not have the means to store fresh air. The CSS *Hunley* torpedoed the USS *Housatonic* on February 17, 1864, with an explosive device at the end of a fifteen-foot pole. When the underwater bomb exploded, it sank not only the Union ship but the *Hunley* as well. The *Housatonic* was the first ship to be sunk by a submarine in combat.

Between the end of the Civil War and the beginning of World War I, the development of new iron warships continued. They operated both above and below the surface of the sea. In 1900 the navy's first combustion electric-powered submarine, the USS *Holland*, was commissioned. It used a gasoline engine when it surfaced and operated on batteries while it was submerged. A diesel engine replaced the gasoline engine in 1912.

This combination of a diesel engine and electric batteries remained the power source for submarines until nuclear power was introduced some fifty years later.

The Dreadnoughts and the Great White Fleet

Ironclads were soon replaced by ships constructed entirely of steel and equipped with more powerful engines and guns

These photographs show the exterior of a German oil-burning submarine (left) and an official in the submarine's engine room (below). In World War I, German submarines were sending 900,000 tons of British ships to the ocean bottom each month.

capable of firing both farther and more accurately. After 1903 huge battleships, called dreadnoughts, became the main battle weapons of the navies of the world.

England, Japan, Germany, and the United States all rushed to build these new battleships. In order to create support for the construction of new dreadnoughts, President Theodore Roosevelt sent the existing American fleet of sixteen battleships, all painted a brilliant white, around the world. In 1908 the "Great White Fleet" visited fourteen countries and not only impressed foreign officials but made it easier to obtain money from Congress to build additional dreadnoughts. By 1909, when Theodore Roosevelt left office, the United States Navy was second in size only to the British Navy.[5]

World War I

When World War I broke out in 1914, it was not the great dreadnoughts that had the most important role of the war at sea but rather the submarines and the destroyers, the small surface warships designed to fight them.

On May 19, 1902, the USS *Decatur* was commissioned and was the first American destroyer put into service. The first destroyers were long and narrow ships, fast and well armed. They were used to protect the huge dreadnoughts from attack by small enemy torpedo boats. Destroyers were also equipped with depth charges and had the task of locating and destroying German submarines.[6]

The American government sent destroyers to England, where they were desperately needed. Shortly after the war had broken out in Europe, nearly one quarter of the British ships had been sunk. German submarines were sending 900,000 tons of British ships to the ocean bottom each month.[7] By July 1917, thirty-four American destroyers were in use by the British. Other American destroyers were being used to surround and protect convoys of merchant ships bringing needed war materials to England. The destroyers quickly stopped more than half of Germany's submarine attacks. They sank enemy submarines, which they found with their echolocation devices and bombed with their depth charges.

World War II

During World War II, submarines and destroyers continued to play a vital role in warfare in both the Atlantic and the Pacific oceans. Battleships twenty or thirty miles away from their targets could still be effective because of their long-range guns. However, battleships played almost no role in the war because of a new weapon, the aircraft carrier. The new aircraft carriers carried airplanes that took off from their decks to bomb the enemy. Almost from the moment that airplanes took to the sky, they were used aboard ships. At first they were used for observation and reconnaissance.

In 1911 an American pilot, Eugene Ely, took off and landed an airplane from a platform constructed on the deck of a cruiser. The British ship HMS *Argus* was the first to have a flight deck that extended the full length of the ship.[8] Soon it became apparent that airplanes could easily defeat surface ships. In July 1921 the United States dropped sixty-seven bombs from airplanes flying over the captured German dreadnought *Ostfriesland* and sank her with sixteen direct hits in front of high-ranking naval observers.[9] By 1922 both Japan and the United States were constructing aircraft carriers.

Pearl Harbor

On December 7, 1941, the Japanese launched hundreds of airplanes from carriers against the United States fleet in Pearl Harbor, Hawaii. They succeeded in destroying or seriously damaging eight battleships, three cruisers, three destroyers, eight other ships, and 188 planes, and they killed or wounded over 3,600 people.[10] The American aircraft carriers were not in port and all of them escaped the surprise attack. President Franklin D. Roosevelt declared war on Japan the next day, and the United States officially entered the war.

Midway

One of the major battles of the war took place on the tiny island of Midway, located west of Pearl Harbor. It was the American possession closest to the islands of

Japan. In May 1942 the Japanese navy sent three fleets of over one hundred ships, including four aircraft carriers, to attack the island. While the Japanese launched their attack against the island on June 4, the Americans attacked the enemy carriers. The battle did not start well for the Americans and they received heavy losses.

A second wave of torpedo bombers from the American carriers USS *Enterprise* and USS *Hornet* found the enemy ships only after the bombers had too little fuel to return to their ships. Nevertheless, they attacked. All of the American planes were shot down. Ensign George H. Gay was the only man to survive the crash landing of his plane in the open sea. He watched as the Americans achieved the greatest naval victory of the war.

The next wave of American aircraft, high-flying bombers, attacked as the Japanese planes were being refueled. They destroyed three of the four

William F. Halsey, Jr. (1882–1959)

A graduate of the Naval Academy in 1904, Bull Halsey became a naval aviator in 1935. In 1940 he was promoted to vice admiral. After Japan attacked Pearl Harbor, Halsey s task force was the only one left in the Pacific area that was operational. In 1942 he was made the commander of the Allied naval forces in the South Pacific. His continued successes against Japan led to his appointment in 1944 as commander of the U.S. Third Fleet. Halsey was appointed fleet admiral in 1945. Two years later, in 1947, he retired.

The Japanese surprise attack on Pearl Harbor on December 7, 1941, destroyed or seriously damaged more than twenty naval vessels, including the USS *Arizona*, shown burning here. The attack, which also killed or wounded over 3,600 people, caused President Franklin D. Roosevelt to declare war on Japan the next day.

Japanese carriers. Planes from the *Hiryu*, the one Japanese carrier not destroyed, struck the American carriers. Bombs and torpedoes left the USS *Yorktown* helpless, and she was abandoned. The next morning more American planes found and destroyed the *Hiryu*. The Americans had won a great victory, destroying four aircraft carriers, two heavy cruisers, four destroyers, and three hundred planes. During the entire battle, neither side's ships confronted the enemy; the entire battle was fought with aircraft.[11]

Navy fighters during the attack on the Japanese fleet off Midway, June 4–6, 1942. In the center can be seen a burning Japanese ship.

D-Day

In 1944, German armies still occupied France and the Netherlands. England, their major enemy in Europe, was across the English Channel, less than a hundred miles away. The Germans knew that any large invasion of Europe would come from England. So the Germans had fortified the coastline of northern France with mines, barbed wire, machine-gun bunkers, and large naval guns.

The Germans were right. In 1943 the Allies decided to invade Europe through France. For over a year, hundreds of thousands of invasion troops were moved to England and thousands of landing craft were moored in ports around the country. During the first days of June 1944, more than one hundred fifty minesweepers cleared the waters off the coast of Normandy of mines. Underwater demolition rangers removed the barbed wire along the beaches.

By four o'clock in the morning on June 6, hundreds of thousands of soldiers were being transferred to small flat-bottomed landing craft from troop transports. Five battleships along with eight cruisers and twenty-two destroyers opened fire against the enemy positions ashore. Around six-thirty, troops began to arrive at beaches along the Normandy coast. The gunfire from the Germans' fortified positions destroyed anything that moved on the beach below. But it was the massive gunfire from the battleships in the channel, directed by British pilots in planes above, that saved the thousands of soldiers pinned down on the beach.

By nightfall more than 63,000 troops were ashore and prepared to attack vital positions farther inland. Over 2,700 ships of the British and American navies took part in this coordinated amphibious landing. It was a tremendous victory for the Allies. The Germans were now forced to fight wars on several fronts at the same time.[12]

Hyman George Rickover
(1900–1986)

Hyman Rickover was born in Poland on January 27, 1900. His family moved to the United States several years later. He graduated from the Naval Academy in 1922 and received a master s degree in electrical engineering from Columbia University in 1927. Then he entered the submarine service. Rickover headed the project to develop the first nuclear-powered submarine, USS *Nautilus*, which was launched in 1954. He is considered the father of the nuclear navy.

Nuclear Power and the Modern Navy

After World War II, there were tremendous advances made in weapons technology. The first great technological advance used by the navy was the adoption of nuclear power for ships, first used in submarines and later on surface warships. On January 17, 1955, the submarine USS *Nautilus* was put to sea for the first time.[13] It was nuclear powered, as great a change for the navy's ships as was the move from sail to steam. On a nuclear ship the fuel

The deck of an aircraft carrier. Today, the major weapon of the navy remains the carrier battle group.

Chester William Nimitz
(1885–1966)

As a young ensign of twenty-two, Chester Nimitz was given the command of the destroyer USS *Decatur*. In 1908 he ran the ship aground and was court-martialed and publicly reprimanded for it. His career survived this setback and at the age of twenty-six, he commanded a division of submarines. He invented a method of refueling ships at sea and commanded the USS *Maumee* during World War I, refueling ships in the middle of the Atlantic Ocean. He was the commander of the cruiser USS *Augusta*, flagship of the U.S. Asiatic Fleet from 1933 to1935. During World War II, he was the Commander in Chief of the Pacific Fleet and Pacific Ocean Operations. Shown is President Franklin Delano Roosevelt in conference with General Douglas MacArthur, Admiral Chester Nimitz, and Admiral W. D. Leahy, while on tour in the Hawaiian Islands.

used to heat the water and create steam is radioactive uranium, which allows a submarine or surface ship to sail for many years before refueling.

On August 3, 1958, the USS *Nautilus* reached the North Pole after an eleven-day submerged voyage. It then continued on, to complete the first Atlantic to Pacific Ocean passage across the top of the world. In twelve weeks, from February 16 to May 10, 1960, another submarine, the USS *Triton*, traveled 36,000 miles around the world submerged except for two short interruptions.

In 1960 submarines were equipped with Polaris missiles. The missiles were designed to be fired from a submerged submarine, rise to the surface, and rocket into the air. The Polaris missile can fly thousands of miles to deliver an atomic bomb on an enemy target. In 1961 the USS *Enterprise*, the first nuclear-powered aircraft carrier, powered by eight nuclear reactors, and the USS *Long Beach*, the first nuclear-powered cruiser, were put into service. In 1962 the USS *Bainbridge*, the first nuclear-powered frigate, joined them.[14]

The Carrier Task Force Today

Today, the major weapon of the navy remains the carrier battle group. Over the last fifty years, carrier task forces have become self-contained, highly powerful, and fast moving. During the conflicts around the world in Vietnam, Iraq, and Bosnia, the United States has deployed carrier battle groups to deliver air power in support of American policy. In places as different as the Gulf of Arabia (Persian Gulf), the South China Sea, and the Mediterranean, carrier battle groups have delivered a superior military presence wherever the United States government needed. Because carriers operate in international waters, their aircraft do not need to secure landing rights on foreign soil. Most carrier battle groups are composed of the same kinds of ships.[15]

At the center of each task force is a Nimitz-class aircraft carrier, accompanied by two guided missile cruisers, a guided missile destroyer, and a frigate, which specialize in antisubmarine warfare; two attack submarines; and a combined ammunition, oiler, and supply ship. A Nimitz-class carrier has a crew of approximately 3,200 seamen and an air wing composed of about 2,500 who fly and maintain the planes. Each carrier deploys about eighty-five aircraft and is powered by two nuclear reactors. A carrier cruises at speeds in excess of thirty miles per hour. All the ships that make up the carrier battle group can also maintain that speed so that the carrier and cruisers can resupply and rearm at full speed in the open ocean.

Joining the Navy

Throughout history, acquiring specific skills or training has usually been accomplished through on-the-job experience. Learning sailing skills through actual practice aboard a ship, where it counts, when it has to be done right, has historically been the way sailors have been trained successfully.

The Apprentice System

Learning by doing under the instruction of a master is called the apprentice system. Before the development of public schools, many jobs were learned this way. In the early days, American sailors all began as apprentices.

Many of these apprentice sailors were teenage boys who were tired of humdrum chores and life at home in general. They longed for new and exciting adventures

Man the GUNS
Join the NAVY

This 1942 poster by McClelland Barclay encouraged Americans to join the navy to support the American cause in World War II. Today, the practical skills learned in the navy can benefit a person throughout his or her future.

in foreign places. Often they would show up at a wharf where a ship was docked and ask if they could sign on. Sometimes a family would arrange for a son to sail with a particular captain as the start of a naval career. If the departure time of a ship approached with the ship badly undermanned, the ship's crew, known as a press-gang, would visit local bars and "press into service," or kidnap, enough men to fill the ship's crew.

By the 1830s the navy had recruiting offices in most of the major seaports along the Atlantic coast. In 1833, Matthew Perry, the younger brother of Oliver Hazard Perry, was appointed commander of the recruiting station in New York. In 1837, he supervised the construction of a steam warship, the USS *Fulton II*, named after Robert Fulton, the inventor of the steamboat. (Fulton himself had designed the first steam warship, the *Demologos*, renamed the *Fulton* after his death.) An entirely new kind of sailor was needed to work on a steamship—a knowledgeable engineer. Perry not only set the standards and pay scale for these new navy engineers but also lobbied hard for the navy to start training its own.

Throughout the rest of the nineteenth century, as the navy replaced its sailing ships with steamships, it upgraded the skills of its sailors. The newly trained sailors had to be able to read instruction manuals and do the mathematical calculations necessary to maintain and repair the machinery used aboard ships.

Matthew Calbraith Perry
(1794–1858)

Commodore Perry was the younger brother of Oliver Hazard Perry, the hero of the Battle of Lake Erie. Matthew Perry also had a long and distinguished career in the navy, fighting pirates in the Mediterranean Sea and the West Indies and slavers off the coast of Africa. He oversaw the construction of the first American steam warship to be used in battle, the USS *Fulton II*, and he is called the father of the American steam navy. He commanded the U.S. naval forces in the Gulf of Mexico during the Mexican War (1846 1848). He led the expedition to Japan (1851 1853) that obtained a treaty opening Japanese ports to American trade.

The Modern Navy

With the development of the more complex electronic and nuclear machinery of the navy in the twenty-first century, prospective sailors are required to have even more skills, such as proficiency in mathematics and logic, than were needed before. Today's naval battles are more likely to be fought with missiles and jet airplanes in which the combatants never see one another.

The qualities that are needed today in the modern navy are not just raw courage and physical strength but quick thinking and deep theoretical knowledge. More and more, even the most common tasks aboard a ship require a strong background in science and technology. The navy needs high school graduates and college-educated people with a successful school record. In order to find competent people, navy recruiters visit high schools, colleges, and job fairs to meet prospective applicants.

Joining Today

The first step recruiters take is to interview the prospective applicant. They ask questions designed to find out whether an individual is suited by nature to life in the military. They also encourage interviewees to ask questions. They talk to potential recruits about the various enlistment options, training programs, and jobs the navy has to offer. With high school students, for example, recruiters may talk about the Delayed Entry Program (DEP), under which individuals sign up before they are ready to report for active duty. This guarantees that a place will be held for them at the school or in the program in which they want to enroll.[1]

Enlistment

The navy has basic requirements. Both men and women must be between seventeen and thirty-four to join. They must also be healthy and be between four feet ten inches and six feet six inches tall. An enlistee must be a United States citizen or have obtained an alien identification number. The service generally encourages young people to finish high school before joining the navy. A high school diploma is required in order to join many of the navy programs.

After recruiters determine that an individual is genuinely interested in joining the navy and meets the basic qualifications, a potential recruit takes the Armed Services Vocational Aptitude Battery test. This not only assesses an applicant's math skills and reading level but is also designed to find out about a person's aptitudes, interests, and natural abilities. There is a minimum test score that must be achieved to join the navy.

Enlistment contracts can be for three, four, five, or six years of active duty. Contracts spell out not only the commitment the individual makes to the navy but also the commitment the navy makes to the individual, specifying the type of training and job he or she will be assigned. Sometimes an enlistment bonus is given as an incentive for signing up for a specific program, such as a medical program or one in advanced electronics or the computer fields.

Naval Reserve

Many people want to serve in the military, even while working a regular job or going to college. For them, the navy offers the option of enlisting in its reserves, which back up the regular navy. Navy recruiters also sign up people for the reserves. The contract to join the Naval Reserve obligates reserve personnel to go through basic training and then commit to reporting for duty one weekend a month and for two full weeks of training each year, usually in the summer.

Crew members from the Air Department of the USS *Theodore Roosevelt* prepare to launch an E-2C "Hawkeye." It is used for early warning of enemy aircraft.

A midshipman prepares to pull down the face curtain that will launch the ejection seat up the track of the ejection seat trainer. Ejection seat training is a part of a one-week aviation training program for students enrolled in the Naval Reserve Officers Training Corps.

Basic Training

When an enlisted man or woman first comes into the navy, he or she reports for basic training, or indoctrination, at the Great Lakes Naval Base in Illinois. This training lasts nine weeks.[2] The first week, upon reporting, recruits are assigned to housing and issued uniforms. Their hair is cut, and doctors and dentists examine them.

Over the next eight weeks, recruits will become accustomed to a whole new way of life. They get used to discipline, obeying orders, and treating superiors with respect. At boot camp, they learn about the navy's traditions. They spend time in the classroom learning about military procedure and naval history. They also spend time outside at close-order drilling, physical exercise, and shipboard simulations.

Every recruit is required to work at a job in the mess hall, such as cleaning tables or peeling potatoes. Everybody takes a swim survival test soon after reporting to boot camp. By the end of basic training, recruits have also learned the basic terms of seamanship and some shipboard skills, such as how to go up and down shipboard ladders. Recruits learn first aid and how to fight fires through actual practice. During basic training, recruits take many written tests. They also have to make it through a "confidence course" before they can graduate.[3]

After the end of basic training and a short leave at home, almost all of the new seamen undertake more training at technical schools around the country. There

Grace Murray Hopper
(1907–1992)

During World War II, Grace Hopper joined the Naval Reserve and was commissioned as a lieutenant, junior grade. She was assigned to the Bureau of Ordnance Computation at Harvard University. Hopper was an expert mathematician, and her skills were used during the war to program the Mark I, the first large computer to be used by the navy. Her team s efforts

resulted in the development of the first widely used computer language, COBOL. In 1983 Hopper was promoted to commodore. At that time she was the oldest commissioned officer in the armed forces of the United States. After her death, a new warship, the USS *Hopper,* was named in her honor.

they will learn a set of job skills so that they can later qualify for a specific position in the navy, such as an electrician or radio technician. Some highly technical jobs, like nuclear propulsion specialist and weapons systems technician, require further training at another school later.[4]

Officers

It is hard enough to train sailors to perform the dangerous and exacting tasks that the entire crew of a ship depend on every day. How do you give officers who command and direct sailors the training and skills to be able to instill in their subordinates duty, loyalty, and courage?

In the early decades of American naval history, officers were trained in much the same way as sailors, through the apprentice system. The navy had a special name for its apprentice officers: It called them midshipmen. They were often the sons and relatives of other naval officers. Midshipmen joined the navy as boys, not yet teenagers. They were entrusted to a ship's captain who was responsible for their general education as well as their naval training.

When he was nine years old, David Glasgow Farragut received his warrant as a midshipman from the secretary of the navy. During the War of 1812, the twelve-year-old Farragut was the youngest person ever to assume command of a vessel of the United States when he was made the captain of a captured British ship, the *Barclay*.[5]

It soon became clear, however, especially after the navy began to grow and needed a substantial number of junior officers, that another way had to be found to find qualified young men to become officers.

U.S. Naval Academy, Annapolis, Maryland

In 1845, President James Polk appointed George Bancroft as secretary of the navy. Bancroft requisitioned an old army post, Fort Severn, in Annapolis, Maryland, for the site of a naval academy to train new officers for the navy. On October 10, 1845, the Naval Academy opened with Franklin Buchanan as its first superintendent. Within a few years, the academy offered not only the basic training in shipboard life, but also a four-year program of college courses equal to a university degree in science and engineering.

Admission to the Naval Academy is through competitive examinations held every year. An applicant must be a United States citizen of good moral character, between seventeen and twenty-three years old, unmarried, not pregnant, and with no dependents. Each applicant must obtain an official nomination to apply. The usual way to receive a nomination is through a member of Congress of the applicant's home state. High scores on competitive tests, a rigorous high school record of achievement, and extracurricular participation within the community are all judged in the selection of the best possible candidates for admission.[6]

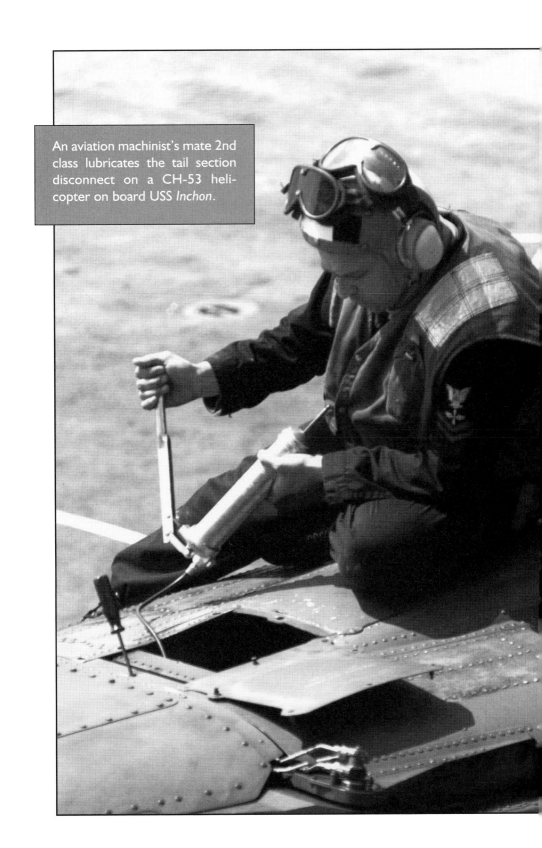

An aviation machinist's mate 2nd class lubricates the tail section disconnect on a CH-53 helicopter on board USS *Inchon*.

James Lawrence
(1781–1813)

On June 1, 1813, naval officer Lawrence, in command of the USS *Chesapeake*, was preparing to sail to the Gulf of St. Lawrence to raid ships bringing supplies to British forces in Canada. Lawrence, disregarding his orders, sailed out of Boston Harbor to answer the challenge of the British frigate, HMS *Shannon*. The two ships traded cannon and rifle fire. Lawrence, mortally wounded in the fighting, ordered his crew, "Don't give up the ship!" The British captured the American ship, but Lawrence's cry soon became the motto of the United States Navy. Shown is the death of Captain Lawrence.

Until the beginning of World War II, graduates of Annapolis formed the majority of new officers each year. While graduation from the academy still ranks as the most prestigious way to become a career officer, today only a small percentage of new naval officers are graduates of Annapolis. The navy needs many more officers each year than any single school can produce. There are a variety of programs that the navy uses to find its new officers.

General Qualifications

All prospective officers must be a United States citizen, be at least nineteen years old (twenty years old to join the Nurse Corps), have a bachelor's degree from an accredited college, and meet the navy's physical standards. The navy actively seeks officer candidates who are adaptable, honest, and mature. They have to be able to work hard, work well with others, be flexible and open-minded, and have the ability to seek new knowledge, think clearly, and draw sound conclusions.

Naval Reserve Officers Training Corps (NROTC)

The Naval Reserve Officers Training Corps Program was established in 1926 to offer the opportunity for young men to qualify for commissions in the United States Naval Reserve while attending college. Later the NROTC was revised to also offer commissions in the regular navy and Marine Corps to NROTC graduates rather than to establish a second naval academy. The

David Glasgow Farragut (1801–1870)

David Farragut was an orphan who was raised by navy hero Master Commandant David Porter. In 1810 Farragut became a midshipman and served during the War of 1812 (1812 1815) aboard the frigate USS *Essex*. When he was twelve years old he was put in charge of a captured ship. Later, he fought pirates in the West Indies. He commanded the naval forces during the Civil War (1861 1865) in the attack on New Orleans, Louisiana (1862), and the defense of Mobile, Alabama (1864). In July 1862 he became the first rear admiral of the navy; in 1864 he became the first vice admiral; and in 1866, the first admiral.

program offers the qualified and motivated student the opportunity to graduate with a bachelor's degree and a commission as either a navy ensign or a second lieutenant in the Marine Corps.

At more than sixty colleges and universities around the country, the navy offers four-year, fully paid scholarships and monthly cash allowances. Those selected for the NROTC earn both bachelor's degrees and commissions as officers in various naval programs. Applicants for the NROTC scholarship program are awarded scholarships through a highly competitive national selection process. The recipient will be commissioned a naval officer upon graduation and is obligated to a minimum of four years active duty in the United States Navy. The scholarship recipient will receive full tuition and other financial benefits including books, class fees, and $150 per month allowance.[7]

Officer Candidate School (OCS)

Officer Candidate School is a thirteen-week course for college graduates at Pensacola, Florida. Application for OCS can be made as early as the second year of college. Admission depends upon the applicant's grades and overall qualifications.

Officer Indoctrination School

Professionals can join the navy as officers in still another way. Officer Indoctrination School is an eight-week course conducted at Newport, Rhode Island. It provides instruction in officer skills to medical, dental, legal, and chaplain personnel. Specialists in the fields of dentistry, medicine, nursing, law, and religion can also be offered direct commissions as officers.

Nuclear Propulsion Officer Candidate Program (NUPOC)

College juniors and seniors who are majoring in physics, chemistry, mathematics, or engineering can apply for the navy's Nuclear Propulsion Officer Candidate Program. They must meet strict academic standards and have completed a year of calculus and calculus-based physics. Those selected then get a monthly cash payment from the navy while receiving special training. When they complete the navy's nuclear prototype training, they also receive a graduation bonus and get a commission.

Aviation Officer Candidate (AOC)

The Aviation Officer Candidate School in Pensacola, Florida, is open to college graduates, including people who have earned degrees beyond a bachelor's. College students can apply for this program as early as their second year in school. After successful completion of the courses offered by the AOC, candidates receive commissions and then attend basic and advanced pilot or naval flight officer training.

Navy Civil Engineer Collegiate Program

College and university students who are majoring in engineering or architecture can also apply to join the

Navy Civil Engineer Collegiate Program during their junior and senior years. The navy pays them a monthly salary while they complete their degrees. Once they graduate, they enroll in Officer Candidate School and then go on for advanced training at the Civil Engineering School at Port Hueneme, California. Civil Engineering School graduates receive commissions as Civil Engineer Corps officers.

Armed Forces Health Professions Scholarship Program (HPSP)

Another scholarship program sponsored by the navy is the Armed Forces Health Professions Scholarship

A Navy lawyer reviews details of a case.

The public works officer for Fleet Hospital Five stands in front of a forklift equipped with a backhoe. The officer supervises about 80 Seabees in support of the hospital and Operation Desert Shield.

Program. Qualified students in medical, pharmacy, osteopathy, dentistry, and optometry schools receive not only a full four-year scholarship but a monthly cash payment as well. After graduation, scholarship recipients go on full-time active duty as navy doctors, pharmacists, osteopaths, dentists, and optometrists.

Judge Advocate General's Corps Student Program (JAG)

One program specifically designed to recruit lawyers for the navy is the Judge Advocate General's Corps Student Program. It offers law students the opportunity to become Naval Reserve commissioned officers while still in school. Once they have graduated and received their attorney's license, having passed their state's bar exam, participants report for active duty service, beginning with nine weeks of training at the Naval Justice School in Newport, Rhode Island.

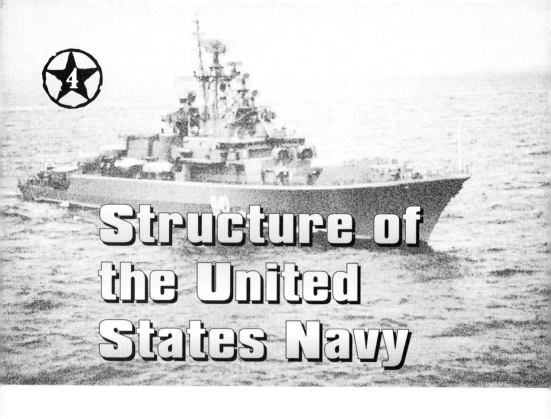

Structure of the United States Navy

There are more than 500,000 people who work for the United States Navy. At the top of the chain of command is the president of the United States.

Commander in Chief

In accordance with the Constitution of the United States, the president is the commander in chief of all of the military. Under the president, the military establishment of the United States is organized first into the Department of Defense. The head of the Department of Defense is the secretary of defense, who is appointed by the president.

Department of Defense

Besides the office of the secretary of defense, the Department of Defense is composed of the

Today more than 500,000 people work for the United States Navy, including the president of the United States, who acts as the commander in chief of all of the military. Here, President Clinton expresses thanks to naval personnel who were deployed overseas in support of NATO Operation Allied Force.

departments of the Army, Navy, and Air Force. The highest-ranking officers of each of the service branches, the Army, Navy, Air Force, and the Marine Corps, are called the Joint Chiefs of Staff. They make up the principal military advisers to the president and the secretary of defense. The highest military rank in the United States is the Chairman of the Joint Chiefs of Staff.

The Navy Department

The secretary of the navy is a civilian who takes orders from the secretary of defense. The secretary of the navy is responsible for the administration, operation, and efficiency of the navy. Under the secretary of the navy is the chief of naval operations, a position that is filled by an officer of the United States Navy.

This chart shows an overview of the organization of the Department of the Navy. The Department of the Navy has three main parts: The Navy Department, consisting of executive offices mostly in Washington, D.C.; the operating forces, including the Marine Corps, the reserve components, and, in time of war, the U.S. Coast Guard; and the shore establishment.[1]

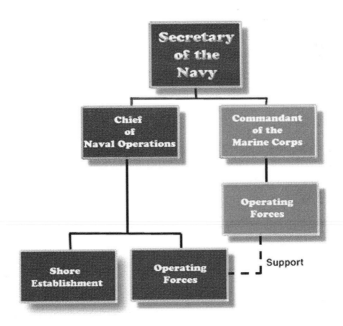

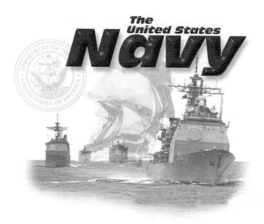

The chief of naval operations (CNO) is the senior military officer in the navy. The CNO is a four-star admiral and is responsible to the secretary of the navy for the command, utilization of resources, and operating efficiency of the operating forces of the navy and of the navy shore activities assigned by the secretary.[2]

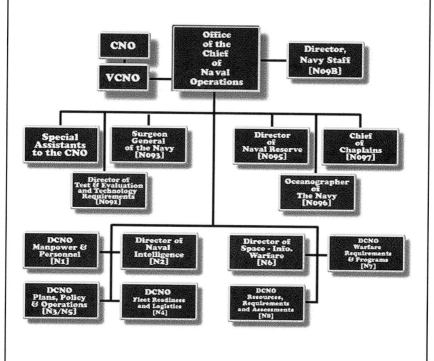

The shore establishment provides support to the operating forces (known as "the fleet") in the form of facilities for the repair of machinery and electronics; communications centers; training areas and simulators; ship and aircraft repair; intelligence and meteorological support; storage areas for repair parts, fuel, and munitions; medical and dental facilities; and air bases.[3]

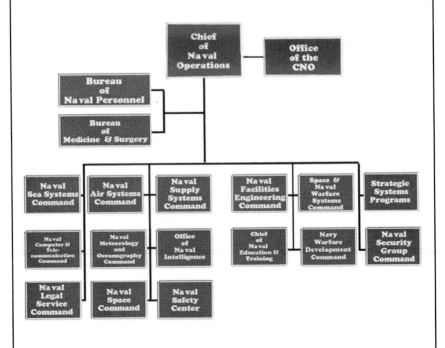

The operating forces' commanders and commanders in chief have a dual chain of command. All navy units also have an administrative chain of command, with the various ships reporting to the appropriate type of commander.[4]

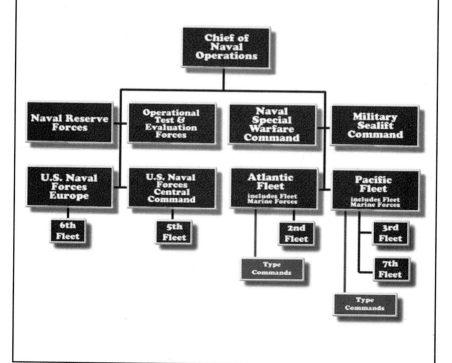

Navy Ranks[5]

Enlisted

Seaman Recruit (E-1)

Seaman Apprentice (E-2)

Seaman (E-3)

Petty Officer 3rd Class (E-4)

Petty Officer 2nd Class (E-5)

Petty Officer 1st Class (E-6)

Chief Petty Officer (E-7)

Senior Chief Petty Officer (E-8)

Master Chief Petty Officer (E-9)

Chief Warrant Officer-2 (WO-2)

Chief Warrant Officer-3 (WO-3)

Chief Warrant Officer-4 (WO-4)

Commissioned Officers

Ensign (O-1)

Lieutenant Junior Grade (O-2)

Lieutenant (O-3)

Lieutenant Commander (O-4)

Commander (O-5)

Captain (O-6)

Flag Officers

Rear Admiral Lower Half (O-7)

Rear Admiral Upper Half (O-8)

Vice Admiral (O-9)

Admiral (O-10)

Fleet Admiral (an honorary position at O-10)

Careers in the Navy

The mission of the navy is to help protect and defend the right of the United States and its allies to move freely on the oceans, to protect American interests, and to provide humanitarian support. In order to do this, the navy depends on more than 750,000 people. Close to half are men and women on active duty. The Naval Reserve includes another 191,000. The navy also employs more than 195,000 civilians. All of these people are given training to become specialists in jobs that the navy requires.

To maintain an effective, ready force, the navy wants to keep these highly trained specialists. To retain these men and women, the navy offers exciting opportunities and benefits to those who make the service their career.

Navy Enlisted Personnel

In 1775 the American navy included mostly ordinary seamen—crew members who sailed the ships and manned the cannons in battles. Almost everyone aboard was expected to be able to perform all of the daily tasks needed to maintain and sail the ship. On most ships only a few men would fill all of the positions on board—the gunner's mate, for example, might also serve as the sergeant at arms and the armorer. These jobs required more specialized skills and more experience than what was required of an ordinary seaman.

As naval ships became larger and the operation of them became more complex, experienced sailors became very important to the navy. It was easier to replace an apprentice seaman than it was to find an experienced gunner's mate. However, most of the specialized jobs were specific to ships—for example, a gunner's mate would have a hard time finding a job other than one aboard a ship. There were few other places his skills and experience were needed. For this reason, the navy did not need to offer attractive retirement benefits to keep its experienced sailors on the job. When the navy started to switch over to steam-powered ships, the picture changed dramatically.

Steamships

In the nineteenth century, those with engineering skills, who could construct or maintain a boiler or a system of gears, were not only needed in the navy, they could get a well-paying job almost anywhere.

By 1839 there were more than seven hundred commercial steamships in the United States alone.[1] Steamships required engineering skills, so the navy began to recruit men with these new skills and officers with engineering training to direct them. New jobs opened up aboard a steamship, such as fireman,

On board an American destroyer. Shown are a five-inch gun and the crew that manned and maintained it. Taken about 1918, during World War I.

machinist, boilermaker, oiler, plumber, and fitter, to name a few. These changes represented the birth of navy engineers, the "Black Gang" as they were called for many years.

In 1879, Thomas A. Edison received the patent for the incandescent light bulb, and within three years, the navy recognized the benefits of this new technology. In 1883 the USS *Trenton* became the first ship of the

On a ship's flight deck, an aviation ordnanceman applies the final wiring to a 2,000-pound laser guided bomb attached to an F-14 "Tomcat" fighter aircraft.

United States Navy to be lit by a system of electric lights.[2]

The navy began what it called its "landsman for training" program in 1899. The navy would take recruits without any maritime background and train them for duty aboard ship.[3] As new inventions and advanced technologies were introduced, the navy created the positions within its job structure to maintain and service them.

Aviation Jobs

There was interest in airplanes as naval weapons as early as 1898, when navy officers were appointed to an interservice board to investigate the military possibilities of aircraft. When the United States entered World War I on April 6, 1917, the navy's aviation force was small; the only air station was at Pensacola, Florida. At that time there were just 163 men assigned to aviation and a total of 54 aircraft. However, by November 11, 1918, the day armistice was declared, the navy's aviation force in Europe alone numbered 1,147 officers and 18,308 enlisted men.

The years following World War I saw a rapid development in aviation. The beginning of the carrier fleet and new aeronautical innovations created the need for new specialists.

World War II saw the development of many kinds of new technologies, such as radar, sonar, cryptoanalysis, and electronic equipment. Each of these required new job skills. It was necessary for the navy to create schools to teach these new skills to its sailors. Today, the navy has one of the largest systems of training schools in the world.

Upon completion of basic training, enlisted personnel undergo specialized training. There are more than fifty thousand different jobs that fall into sixty different fields within the United States Navy. These include fields such as electronics, engineering, computer technology, nuclear propulsion, and aviation.[4] Some of these jobs involve skills that can easily be applied in civilian life as well as in the navy. They offer ex-sailors a head start to get good jobs when they leave the navy. Some of these specialties include air traffic

U.S. Navy Captain Robert D. Jenkins III (right), commanding officer of the USS *Philippine Sea*, discusses his ship's position in relation to other yet unidentified surface contacts with the ship's tactical officer.

controller, computer programmer, computer repair technician, gas turbine engine mechanic, journalist, photographer, surveyor, and welder.[5] There are some skills, however, that are so specialized that civilian jobs requiring them are few.

Nuclear Jobs

Enlisted personnel can receive training and work in both nuclear energy and nuclear propulsion in the navy. This training typically takes more than eighteen months.

Nuclear power is used on aircraft carriers, cruisers, frigates, and submarines. The service boasts that it has "an outstanding safety record [due to] the world's finest nuclear power training."[6]

After going through recruit training, enlisted personnel enter a second phase of training at the Naval Nuclear Power Training Command in Charleston, South Carolina. Recruits go on to Nuclear Power School for six months of academic work. For a fourth phase of training, students join one of two Nuclear Power Training Units (NPTUs), going to either a prototype nuclear power plant or a permanently moored nuclear-powered submarine. Sailors in the nuclear field can then work as engineering lab technicians or welders. Some become instructors. Nuclear program participants are eligible for rapid advancement through ratings, enlistment bonuses, special duty assignment pay, and large selective reenlistment bonuses of up to $45,000.[7]

Other Enlisted Benefits

The navy offers its sailors a number of other benefits that make a career in the navy attractive. One is the opportunity to see the world. Over the course of a career, most sailors get a chance to see many countries and cross both the equator and the international date line. All personnel receive a salary that is guaranteed by their enlistment contracts. Cash bonuses are offered for reenlistment in certain job fields that are considered critical to the navy.

Sailors earn thirty days of paid vacation each year. Regular promotions bring greater salaries as well as greater responsibilities. The navy offers all of its personnel housing, housing allowances, and meals free. All of the medical and dental care for people on active duty is also provided at no cost to them. Low-cost shopping for food and material goods is provided at exchanges and commissaries. Free or low-cost entertainment is offered. Advanced education and training is available, usually free of charge or sometimes at low cost. The navy provides a close-knit community and provides for almost all the needs for its personnel.

After twenty years of service, enlisted personnel become eligible for retirement. Someone who enters the navy at eighteen is therefore eligible for retirement when he or she is under forty years old. Such retirees will receive a retirement check for life, providing financial security for their families at a time when they are still young enough to begin a second career.

Married servicemen who live off the base enjoy all of these benefits as well as a monthly allowance for their family's housing and meals. Medical and dental care for everyone in the family is also provided at low cost. One of the most important benefits is often undervalued—schools on military bases generally outperform schools in civilian life. Many people in the service and their families look on the military life as a superior lifestyle, preferable to regular civilian life.

Officers

Officers in the navy are divided into three categories: unrestricted line officers, restricted line officers, and staff corps officers.

Unrestricted Line Officers

Unrestricted line officers perform their duties in surface ships, submarines, and aircraft. One kind of unrestricted line officer, the special warfare officer, leads sea-air-land (SEAL) teams in special reconnaissance, harbor clearing, and intelligence missions. Another category of unrestricted line officer is a special operations officer, who serves in diving, salvage, and explosive ordnance jobs.

Unrestricted line officers on surface ships are called surface warfare officers (SWOs). They manage all of the operations aboard surface ships not only on the primary navy warships, including the nuclear-powered aircraft carriers, cruisers, and frigates, but also on support ships, such as stores ships, minesweepers, rescue ships, and salvage ships. These positions are open to both men and women. The goal of all surface warfare officers is to have command of a ship at sea. All ship commanders are called captain and are in complete control of the life of the ship and its crew. Becoming captain is usually the last step in a series of assignments, each requiring more experience and expertise.

Unrestricted line officers who serve on submarines are in a class of their own. After they are commissioned

Included in the U.S. Navy's many highly trained specialists are the sea-air-land teams, or SEALs. They specialize in reconnaissance, harbor clearing, and intelligence missions.

as line officers, those selected for submarine service attend nuclear power school and submarine school. Then they are assigned to either a nuclear-powered fast attack or a ballistic missile submarine. These officers' career at sea is almost always in submarines, and their primary goal, like the officers aboard surface ships, is to command a submarine at sea as its captain.

Unrestricted line officers in the air are either naval aviators, pilots who fly navy aircraft, or naval flight officers, who control the advanced weapons and guidance systems on the aircraft. After receiving their commissions, prospective aviation officers receive assignments to primary flight training schools and, upon completion, to advanced flight training schools.

Restricted Line Officers

Restricted line officers, who are not eligible to command ships at sea, perform duties according to their special skills. These restricted line officers include aerospace engineers, nuclear power instructors, naval reactor engineers, intelligence officers, public affairs officers, and cryptologists (code breakers).

Staff Corps Officers

The third type of navy officer is a staff corps officer, which include chaplains, lawyers, dentists, doctors, and nurses. Staff corps officers of the United States Navy also serve in the Marine Corps and the Coast Guard.

Two midshipmen at Annapolis.

Officers' Benefits

Career navy officers enjoy most of the same benefits as their counterparts among the enlisted—regular advances in salary and responsibility, a chance to see the world, equal treatment regardless of race or gender, and thirty days of paid vacation each year. In addition, officers enjoy recreational facilities and officers' clubs and have opportunities to take part in the Postgraduate Educational Program, which provides help in earning a master's or doctoral degree, and the Defense Language Institute in Monterey, California, which provides instruction in over fifty languages. Perhaps the best benefit of a career as an officer or an enlisted man or woman in the navy is the self-respect one gains in being a part of the prestigious worldwide team of professional sailors.

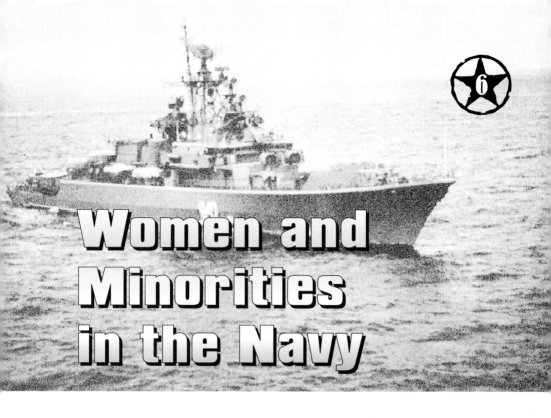

Women and Minorities in the Navy

Today the navy is an equal opportunity employer. It recruits people regardless of race or gender. Women are joining the navy in great numbers; the only two programs that they are not eligible to join are submarine duty and Special Warfare (SEALs). There is also a greater percentage of African Americans in the navy than in the general population of the United States. However, this was not always so.

No Women on Board!

For a little more than a hundred years after its beginning, the navy had no female personnel. In fact, naval regulations in 1802 stated that women could not even travel as passengers on navy ships unless orders were issued allowing them to do so. Occasionally, navy officers received permission to take their wives, their

daughters, or their sisters with them on an assignment.

In the 1830s, Commodore Charles Stewart took his wife and daughter with him when he commanded the American naval squadron off the Pacific coast of South America. Midshipman Stuyvesant Fish recorded in his journal that the sailors did not like having the Stewart women on board. He wrote: "The females have been already wished home a thousand times by every officer, as they have already given difficulty and will cause, eventually, the cruise to be disagreeable. They rule when the ship is to sail, already."[1]

Women in the Naval Reserve

Just before the United States entered World War I, Secretary of the Navy Josephus Daniels decided to make the Naval Reserve open to women. The service desperately needed clerks and stenographers, called yeomen in the navy. Looking back twenty-five years later, Daniels remembered: "'Is there any law that says a yeoman must be a man?' I asked my legal advisers. The answer is that there was not . . . 'Then enroll women in the Naval Reserve as yeomen,' I said, 'and we will have the best clerical assistance the country can

A nurse records information on a medical chart aboard the hospital ship *Comfort*, deployed to the Persian Gulf during Operation Desert Storm.

provide.'"[2] Women were then recruited for the Naval Coast Defense Reserve.

Once the United States entered the war in 1917, the navy actively searched for women to recruit. The addition of women allowed more men to enter active service. By the time the armistice was signed in 1918, 11,275 female yeomen had been recruited. They did most of the clerical work for the Department of the Navy, as well as serving as translators, draftsmen, fingerprint experts, camouflage designers, and recruiters. Five women had been sent to France with hospital units. One worked in the Office of Naval Intelligence in Puerto Rico. Female yeomen also went to Guam, the Panama Canal Zone, and Hawaii.[3] After the war the navy discharged its female yeomen. There were no more, as of December 1919.[4]

Navy Nurses

Women were first allowed to join the navy as nurses as early as the War of 1812. However, they were volunteers. In 1908, Congress passed a law establishing the Navy Nurse Corps. The law provided for the appointment of a superintendent and "as many chief nurses, nurses, and reserve nurses as may be needed." They all had to be graduates of hospital training schools and to have studied nursing for at least two years. They also had to demonstrate "professional, moral, mental and physical fitness."[5] In World War I, female navy nurses worked in hospitals or on ambulance ships.

Winifred Quick Collins
(1918–)

Winifred Quick Collins was one of the very first women to join up after Congress authorized the formation of the WAV E S Women Accepted for Voluntary Emergency Service. She was commissioned as an ensign. In 1948 she was one of five hundred women commissioned in the regular peacetime navy. She had a navy career spanning more than thirty years, rising through the ranks to become a captain. In the 1960s and 1970s she helped establish navy policy that opened more opportunities to women.

When the United States entered World War II in December 1941, the Navy Nurse Corps was ready. Navy nurses were among those who witnessed the Japanese bombing of Pearl Harbor. Some were captured during the Japanese invasion of the Philippines. By the end of the war, there were 11,000 navy nurses in uniform.[6] The corps functioned unlike other sections of the navy. For more than thirty years, navy nurses were awarded no rating. In 1942, however, President Franklin D. Roosevelt signed into law an act granting them rank corresponding to regular commissioned officers. Their superintendent, Sue Dauser, who had then served in the corps for twenty-five years, became the equivalent of a lieutenant commander.[7]

WAVES

On July 30, 1942, Public Law 689 went into effect, establishing a Women's Reserve, a separate branch of the Naval Reserve. The law specifically stated that its purpose was to free men for duty at sea and that women reservists would be used only for shore duty in the continental United States. It also stipulated that women reservists were not to spend more than $200 on uniforms and equipment![8]

Women reservists would be known as WAVES, Women Accepted for Voluntary Emergency Service. When the law passed, 119 women immediately signed up.[9] On October 19, 1944, the navy issued a press release stating that as of that date African-American women would also be accepted in the Women's Reserve.[10]

Petty Officer 3rd Class Rosalie Burton operates a training device designed to simulate in-flight pressure changes on aviators. She operates, maintains, and teaches about navy training equipment at the Naval Aerospace Medicine Institute.

Below: During World War II, women took over many of the jobs traditionally held by men to support the war effort on the home front.

Right: Today's navy offers women many new opportunities. Shown is Ensign Matice Wright, the first African-American woman to become a naval flight officer.

By the end of the war, the navy included more than 80,000 WAVES working in 900 different jobs. This included 8,000 officers and 76,000 enlisted women. At that time, there were another 8,000 in training.[11] WAVES also served in the Korean and Vietnam wars. In 1956 legislation was enacted that proclaimed women as part of the regular

United States Navy, making the WAVES a unique group of women.

Women in the Navy Today

Today, women are part of all navy operations. There were 3,700 navy women who were deployed to the Persian Gulf during Operation Desert Storm. Speaking of the 37,000 military women involved in the theater of operations, a Department of Defense report concluded: "Women performed admirably and without substantial friction or special considerations."[12] At sea, navy women served on hospital, supply, oiler, and ammunition ships. On land, they served in construction crews, fleet hospitals, and air reconnaissance squadrons, as well as filling other support billets.

African Americans in the Navy

Since the Revolutionary War, African Americans have served in the navy. They made up between 6 and 10 percent of navy personnel during the War of 1812. Many were crewmen on board Oliver H. Perry's ships at the Battle of Lake Erie.

During the Civil War, the navy included over 30,000 sailors who were African Americans, approximately 25 percent of the force.[13] Robert Smalls was an African-American naval hero of the Civil War.[14] He

"above and beyond the call of duty"

DORIE MILLER
*Received the Navy Cross
at Pearl Harbor, May 27, 1942*

commandeered a Confederate armed frigate, the *Planter*, and delivered it to the Union forces. African Americans also served in large numbers in the navy during the Spanish-American War. In fact, throughout the nineteenth century, African Americans made up between 25 and 30 percent of the navy's enlisted personnel. However, after 1900, their role was substantially reduced. They began to be allowed to work only in galleys or engine rooms.[15]

In World War I, the navy included just 6,750 African-American men, who were used chiefly as wardroom attendants. There were also twenty-four African-American women in the Naval Reserve. After 1919 the navy stopped enlisting African Americans, although a few African Americans continued to act as gunner's mates, torpedo men, and machinists because reenlistment in such specialties had never been banned.[16] By 1932 there were 441 African-American sailors in the navy, less than one percent of all navy personnel.[17]

By June 1940 this number had increased almost tenfold, rising to 4,007.[18] Of this number, just six were regular-rated seamen. The other 4,001 served as steward's mates. Regardless of their jobs aboard ship, everybody, including stewards, got a battle station

A Navy recruitment poster celebrating the heroism of Doris (Dorie) Miller. Miller was the first African American to win the Navy Cross, and his heroic story helped end segregation in the Navy.

African Americans have served in the Navy since the Revolutionary War, but it took until the end of World War II for racial barriers to truly begin to fall. Today, the navy stands alongside the other military branches of the United States as an equal opportunity employer. The midshipman pictured here is enrolled in the Naval Reserve Officers Training Corps.

assignment. On the very first day of the American participation in World War II, at Pearl Harbor, steward Doris Miller performed heroically on board the burning and sinking battleship USS *Arizona*. He manned a machine gun to destroy two enemy planes. Miller's heroism was widely publicized and led to greater participation of African Americans in the navy during the war.[19]

World War II

African-American leaders tried to create support for civil rights during World War II. The press launched what it called the Double V campaign, calling for victory over fascism abroad and segregation laws at home. The Committee for Negro Participation in the National Defense Program lobbied for the opening of the armed services to African Americans. As a result, two amendments to

J. Paul Reason (1943–)

Joseph Paul Reason, the navy s first African-American four-star admiral, was born in Washington, D.C., in 1943. After graduating from the Naval Academy at Annapolis, he served on the nuclear-powered missile cruiser USS *Truxtun* and the nuclear-powered aircraft carrier USS *Enterprise*. He served a two-year assignment as the naval aide to President Jimmy Carter, followed by other assignments at sea, including captain of the nuclear-powered guided missile cruiser USS *Bainbridge*. In 1994 he was assigned as deputy chief of Naval Operations, a post he held until President William Clinton nominated him as a four-star admiral and assigned him to be the Commander in Chief of the Atlantic Fleet.

the Selective Service Act of 1940 guaranteed minorities the right to enlist and allowed them to be drafted. It said that "there shall be no discrimination against any person on account of race or color."[20] However, all this meant was that African Americans were allowed in the services; the services remained segregated.

Secretary of the Navy Frank Knox believed that African Americans could not be integrated into regular navy units. He said he feared that racial prejudice might cause ships' crews to be "impaired in efficiency."[21] While President Franklin D. Roosevelt agreed

Aviation Boatswain's Mate 1st Class Anthony Logan and Airman Harry Settles operate search and recovery equipment in the catapult control room of the aircraft carrier *Saratoga* during Operation Desert Shield.

that it would be difficult to integrate the navy fully during wartime, he saw integration as a reasonable goal. He believed that if African Americans sailed on warships, all could learn to know one another and "then we can move on from there."[22]

In 1942 the navy acted on the Selective Service Act's antidiscrimination clause and announced it would enlist 14,000 African-American men in the general service. It quickly set up segregated training facilities. At first, relatively few African Americans volunteered for the navy, choosing the army instead. The navy then assigned specialists to the recruitment program for African Americans, and the program expanded quickly.

After February 1943 men between the ages of eighteen and thirty-eight were taken into the military only through Selective Service (the draft). The Bureau of Naval Personnel set quotas, aiming to draft about 2,700 African-American men every month. The navy ultimately agreed to draft 125,000 African Americans by January 1944. President Roosevelt wanted African-American participation in the war effort to match the makeup of the population; 10 percent of the navy was to be African American, just as 10 percent of the population was. Twenty-seven African-American Naval Construction Battalions (CBs, or Seabees) were established. Seabees worked on projects such as building roadways, bridges, and airstrips, in addition to fighting the enemy.

In general, African Americans in the navy during World War II experienced great dissatisfaction; they wanted to fight and were frustrated by segregation. In 1943 there were no African-American officers in the navy, and despite complaints by Eleanor Roosevelt, the wife of President Franklin D. Roosevelt, African-American women were barred from inclusion in the Navy Nurse Corps.

Toward the end of the war, the navy's Special Programs Unit achieved a small victory when two hundred African-American enlisted men were assigned to the USS *Masin*, a destroyer escort. In March 1944,

In 1943 there were no African-American officers in the navy, and despite complaints by Eleanor Roosevelt, the wife of President Franklin D. Roosevelt, African-American women were barred from inclusion in the Navy Nurse Corps.

thirteen African Americans were commissioned as officers in the United States Navy. They would serve aboard the all–African-American combat vessels.

By the end of World War II, racial barriers were falling. African Americans received more seagoing assignments as well as submarine and aviation training. African-American women were being recruited as nurses. In August 1945 there were 164,942 African Americans enlisted in the navy, including 60 African-American officers. One of them was Ensign Samuel Gravely, who would later become the navy's first African-American admiral.

There were still many inequalities in the treatment of the different races within the navy, but the navy was determined to correct them. In 1944 the Bureau of Naval Personnel published a pamphlet, *Guide to the Command of Negro Naval Personnel*, which acknowledged problems in the segregated navy: "The idea of compulsory racial segregation is disliked by almost all Negroes, and literally hated by many. This antagonism is in part a result of the fact that as a principle it embodies a doctrine of racial inferiority. It is also a result of the lesson taught the Negro by experience that in spite of the legal formula of 'separate but equal' facilities, the facilities open to him under segregation are in fact usually inferior as to location or quality."[23]

Today, the navy stands alongside the other military branches of the United States as an equal opportunity employer. In 1992 there was a greater percentage of African Americans in the navy than in the general population. However, African-American officers accounted for little more than 4 percent of all officers at the time. One of the reasons is that African Americans make up less than 6 percent of all college graduates, so the available pool of officer candidates is small. The navy set a goal to raise the number of African-American officers to 6 percent by the year 2000.[24]

Studies show that those in the military consider their environment to be fairer and less discriminatory than others in civilian life. This attitude is the most concrete proof of the growing racial equality in the navy today.

The Future

In the future the United States Navy will continue to perform its primary mission of protecting the United States. With an approach called network-centric warfare, which utilizes satellite technology and intelligence-gathering capabilities, the navy can spot the buildup of aggressive weapons and military forces anywhere in the world. If the United States cannot prevent aggression, it will at least be in a position to defeat it quickly with little loss of men and equipment.

In addition, the modern navy will contribute to the achievement of other political goals of the United States. In an era when there are many world crises, the presence of navy carrier task forces enables the United States to help maintain the peace among other nations. Other political goals in which the navy has a role are to encourage the spread of democracy and the respect for human rights in all the nations of the world.[1]

Plans for the Near Future

Navy officials often express concern over funding to modernize its equipment. Although in the coming years the navy projects that it will have twelve carrier battle groups, twelve amphibious ready groups, ten active carrier wings, and one reserve carrier wing, the navy will actually have shrunk. The navy has plans to reduce the number of surface combatant ships from 128 to 116 and attack submarines from 73 to 50. Although at the times when war or the threat of war looms, peacetime plans can change and change rapidly. Being prepared in times of national emergency is always a constant concern.[2]

The ability of the navy to reduce its overall size and still maintain an adequate readiness depends upon the replacement of older equipment with new, technologically advanced systems. These systems are very costly. The navy is faced with the task of becoming smaller but at an increased cost. The success of such a program can only happen if the navy can inform the public and the United States Congress of the necessity to retain a high level of funding for the American armed forces.

Future Personnel Needs

Like other branches of the American military, the navy sees that one of its biggest challenges is to have enough motivated, experienced, and skilled personnel to maintain and operate its equipment. Retaining the skilled and experienced people it has is half of the challenge; the other half is recruiting and training enough new,

Since its beginning, the United States Navy has relied as much on the courage and dedication of its sailors as it has on the ever-growing technology of its equipment.

young people who have the potential to fill the navy's needs in the twenty-first century.

Many jobs will become vacant because of either the retirement of career sailors or the desire of those who complete an enlistment contract to accept positions in the civilian workforce. Although over the next ten years the navy expects to cut its size by 18,000 active, 4,100 reserve, and 8,400 civilian employees, it still expects having difficulty filling the remaining positions with qualified people.

The American economy is presently strong, unemployment in the civilian sector is low, and pay in civilian jobs is high. Fewer Americans now want to join an armed service than at other times in the history of the United States. The navy reports that it is having a hard time keeping trained and experienced sailors once they have joined the service. Long tours of duty away from home keep families apart and are generally unpopular with married sailors.

The Department of the Navy has pledged to seek from Congress approval for higher pay and better retirement packages for its men and women in the hopes that this will retain more navy personnel. It is a vital challenge that must be met. Ever since the beginning of the United States Navy, the courage and dedication of its sailors has been responsible for its success. So it will be in the future.

Weapons, Technology, and Ships

Aircraft Carrier

In 1911 the American flier Eugene Ely took off and landed on platforms erected on the deck of a cruiser. In 1918 the British ship HMS *Argus* had a landing deck placed over its entire length. During the 1920s, most of the world's naval powers began to build aircraft carriers as support vessels for battleships. The decisive American victory at the Battle of Midway in World War II was a battle in which the ships on each side did not confront their enemy. Today, aircraft carrier task forces are the major weapons of the surface navy.

Ballistic Missile Submarine

In 1954, soon after their invention, nuclear submarines were equipped with missiles that could be launched while the submarine remained underwater. They could travel thousands of miles to deliver atomic bombs accurately to predetermined targets. At present there is no known effective weapon against them.

Battleship

The battleship was developed around the 1850s when the hulls of warships were covered with armor to protect them against cannon fire. The powerful battleship

Aircraft carrier

could defeat almost any other type of ship for many years. It got its name as a "line-of-battle" ship when ships preparing for combat sailed in a column formation. After World War II many battleships were decommissioned as a result of the development of missiles that were more effective than the most powerful guns on ships.

Destroyer

Originally, destroyers were vessels armed with cannons to protect ships from torpedo boats, but they were soon fitted with torpedoes, as they were more effective in the rough seas than the smaller torpedo boats. To

Tomahawk cruise missile

Tomahawk cruise missile launched from a destroyer.

add to their effectiveness, destroyers were made larger and were fitted with powerful antiaircraft guns. During World War II, destroyers provided protection for large fleets of ships. After World War II the destroyer was used for missile launching and for anti-submarine attacks.

Ironclad

Ironclad was the early name for warships covered with iron plates as protection against cannon fire. The first true ironclad was the French ship *Gloire*, launched in 1859. During the American Civil War, the ironclad Confederate ship CSS *Virginia* met the Union ironclad USS *Monitor* in the first battle between iron ships. Neither ship suffered much damage in the battle.

Nuclear-Powered Submarine

In 1948 the United States Atomic Energy Commission gave a contract to the Westinghouse Electric Company to develop a nuclear propulsion plant suitable for installation in a submarine. On June 14, 1952, the construction of the USS *Nautilus* was begun. Successful trials of the new submarine, named for the submarine in Jules Verne's novel *20,000 Leagues Under the Sea*, were completed in 1954, and the new weapon was put into operation. Today nuclear-powered submarines can operate at maximum speeds underwater for months at a time.

Nuclear-powered submarine

Radar

Radar, an acronym of *RA*dio *D*irection *A*nd *R*ange, is a method of detecting unseen objects by sending out radio waves, which bounce off solid objects in their path and return to the radar receiver. The length of time it takes for the radio waves to return is used to determine the distance of the unseen object. The direction of the returning radio waves determines the location of the unseen object. During World War II, radar was used by U.S., British, French, and German forces to detect enemy submarines and airplanes.

Revolving Turret

During the age of sailing ships, cannons were placed in fixed positions along the sides of the ship. To fire

Revolving turret

cannons, the entire ship had to be turned to face the target. During the American Civil War, John Ericsson developed a huge rotating turret that carried a cannon for the main deck of the USS *Monitor*, one of the first ironclad warships. The rotating turret allowed the *Monitor* to fire its cannon in any direction and gave it a great advantage over fixed guns.

Screw Propeller

The propeller is the rotating screw of a steamship, which forces a steamship through the water. The first mechanical device used aboard steamships for this purpose was the paddle wheel, which was ineffective when the ship rolled in the waves of the sea. A device was

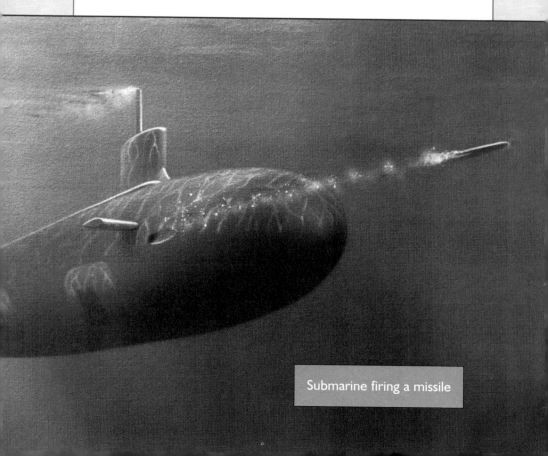

Submarine firing a missile

needed that would remain below the water in even the roughest seas. The first propellers had only two blades, but more efficient three-and four-bladed ones quickly were developed.

Sonar

Sonar, an acronym of *SO*und *N*avigation *A*nd *R*anging, is a method of detecting objects underwater by sending pulses of high-energy sound waves through the water, which bounce off solid objects and return to the sonar receiver. The length of time it takes for the sonar waves to return is used to determine the distance of the unseen object. The direction of the returning sonar waves determines the location of the unseen object. Sonar was developed as an antisubmarine weapon by the British during the 1920s and installed on all British destroyers by 1932. Sonar proved to be a decisive aid in defeating the German and Japanese submarines during World War II.

Steam Power

In 1802 the world's first successful boat powered by a steam engine, the HMS *Charlotte Dundas*, was tested in Scotland. In 1807, Robert Fulton in the United States oversaw the construction of the merchant steamship USS *Clermont*, which was propelled by British steam engines and used to transport cargoes up and down the Hudson River. On October 29, 1814, the USS *Demologos*, the first steam-powered warship, also designed by Robert Fulton, was launched in New

York Harbor. *The Demologos* was renamed *Fulton the First* after Fulton's death. Gradually all warships became steam powered and remain so today.

Torpedo

The torpedo, named after the torpedo eel, which gives an electric shock if touched, was originally a mine, a barrel filled with gunpowder that exploded when touched. In 1867, Robert Whitehead of England invented a self-propelled, eel-shaped, underwater missile that contained dynamite in its head and was called a torpedo. A Whitehead torpedo claimed its first victim in the Russo-Turkish War of 1878. By 1914 torpedoes were used aboard submarines, and they proved an effective weapon against surface vessels during World War II.

Chapter Notes

Chapter 1. "We Have Met the Enemy and They Are Ours"

1. William Jeffrey Welsh and David Curtis Skaggs, *War on the Great Lakes: Essays Commemorating the 175th Anniversary of the Battle of Lake Erie* (Kent, Ohio: Kent State University Press, 1991), pp. 5–36; E. B. Potter, *The Naval Academy Illustrated History of the United States Navy* (New York: Thomas Y. Crowell Company, 1971), pp. 50–54; Samuel Eliot Morison, "Old Bruin": *Commodore Matthew C. Perry, 1794–1858* (Boston: Little, Brown and Company, 1967), pp. 41–49.

2. "Status of the United States Navy." *United States Navy Page*. n.d. <http://www.chinfo.Navy.mil/navpalib/news/.www/status.html> (April 23, 2000).

Chapter 2. History of the United States Navy

1. Wilbur Cross, *Naval Battles and Heroes* (New York: American Heritage Publishing Co., 1960), p. 23.

2. Peter Booth Wiley, *Yankees in the Land of the Gods* (New York: Viking, 1990), pp. 54–56.

3. Stephen Howarth, *To Shining Sea: A History of the United States Navy, 1775–1991* (New York: Random House, 1991), pp. 184–185.

4. Ibid., p. 188.

5. Ibid., pp. 280–288.

6. John C. Reilly, Jr., *United States Destroyers of World War II* (Poole, England: Blandford Press, 1983), pp. 9–10.

7. Cross, p. 114.

8. Peter Kemp, ed., *The Oxford Companion to Ships and the Sea* (London: Oxford University Press, 1988), p. 12.

9. Howarth, p. 333.

10. Ibid., p. 390.

11. Cross, pp. 133–135.

12. James M. Morris, *History of the US Navy* (New York: Exeter Books, 1987), p. 162.

13. "Frequently Asked Questions: Ratings and the Evolution of Jobs in the Navy." *Naval Historical Center Page*. June 1, 1999. <http://www.history.navy.mil/faqs/faq78-1.htm> (April 23, 2000); Howarth, p. 494.

14. Howarth, pp. 494–496.

15. "The Carriers." *United States Navy Page*. n.d. <http://www.chinfo.navy.mil/navpalib/ships/carriers/> (April 23, 2000).

Chapter 3. Joining the Navy

1. "Today's Navy: Let the Journey Begin," United States Navy brochure 611-234, n.d., p. [6].

2. "Frequently Asked Questions." *Navy Jobs Page*. n.d. <http://www.navyjobs.com/html/highschool/faq.htm#question7> (December 11, 1999).

3. "Basic Training Curriculum." *Great Lakes Page*. n.d. <http://www.ntcpao.com/basic.html> (April 9, 2000).

4. "Today's Navy: Let the Journey Begin."

5. Leland P. Lovette, *School of the Sea* (New York: Frederick A. Stokes Company, 1941), p. 13.

6. "Naval Academy Basic Eligibility." *United States Naval Academy Page*. n.d. <http://www.usna.edu/Admissions/require.htm> (April 23, 2000).

7. "NROTC Recruitment." *University of North Carolina at Chapel Hill Naval Reserve Officers Training Corps Page*. n.d. <http://www.unc.edu/depts/nrotc/> (April 23, 2000); "NROTC Scholarship Information." *University of Texas at Austin Naval Reserve Officers Training Corps Page*. n.d. <http://Navy.rotc.utexas.edu/applying.html> (April 23, 2000).

Chapter 4. Structure of the United States Navy

1. "Navy Organization: An Overview." *United States Navy Page*. n.d. <www.chinfo.navy.mil/navpalib/organization/org-over.html> (March 27, 2001).

2. "Navy Organization: Office of the Chief of Naval Operations." *United States Navy Page*. n.d. <www.chinfo.navy.mil/navpalib/organization/org-cno. html> (March 27, 2001).

3. "Navy Organization: The Shore Establishment." *United States Navy Page*. n.d. <www.chinfo.navy.mil/navpalib/organizationorg-shor.html> (March 27, 2001).

4. "Navy Organization: The Operating Forces." *United States Navy Page*. n.d. <www.chinfo.navy.mil/navpalib/organization/orgopfor.html> (March 27, 2001).

5. "Navy Ranks." Based on the *NJROTC Field Manual*, 4th ed. (NAVEDTRA 37116-D), pp. 4-1–4-3. *N. Myrtle Beach High School NJROTC Page*. n.d. <http://www.hcs.k12.sc.us/high/nmbh/99-00/school/curricula/jrotc/page7.html> (April 19, 2000).

Chapter 5. Careers in the Navy

1. Stephen Howarth, *To Shining Sea: A History of the United States Navy, 1775–1991* (New York: Random House, 1991), p. 145.

2. "Frequently Asked Questions: Ratings and the Evolution of Jobs in the Navy." *Naval Historical Center Page*. June 1, 1999. <http://www.history.navy.mil/faqs/faq78-1.htm> (April 23, 2000); Howarth, p. 494.

3. Paul Stillwell, ed., *The Golden Thirteen* (Annapolis, Md.: Naval Institute Press, 1993), p. xviii.

4. *Navy Jobs Page*. <http://www.navyjobs.com/html/about.htm> (April 23, 2000).

5. *Navy Jobs Page*. <http://www.navyjobs.com/highschool/html/sub_60fields.html> (April 23, 2000).

6. *Navy Jobs Page.* <http://www.navyjobs.com/highschool/html/sub_nuclear.html> (April 23, 2000).

7. Ibid.

Chapter 6. Women and Minorities in the Navy

1. Alma R. Lawrence, "History of Women on Navy Ships in the Nineteenth Century." Memo dated February 23, 1951. Operational Archives Branch. *Naval Historical Center Page.* <www.history.navy.mil/faqs/faq48-3a.htm> (April 23, 2000).

2. Ibid.

3. Ibid.

4. Winifred Quick Collins with Herbert M. Levine, *More Than a Uniform: A Navy Woman in a Navy Man's World* (Denton, Tex.: University of North Texas Press, 1997), p. xiii.

5. "Establishment of Navy Nurse Corps, Public Law No. 115, 13 May 1908." Extract from *The Statutes at Large of the United States of America from December 1907 to March 1909*, vol. 35, pt. 1 (Washington, D.C.: U.S. Government Printing Office, 1909). *Naval Historical Center Page.* <www.history.nav.mil/faqs/faq48-3c.htm> (December 7, 1999).

6. "What Is a Wave?" *WAVES National Page.* n.d. <http://wavesnational.hypermart.net/waves.htm> (April 23, 2000).

7. Ibid.

8. "Establishment of Women's Reserve, Public Law 689, H. R.6807, 30 July 1942 [Chapter 538]." *Naval Historical Center Page.* <http://www.history.navy.mil/faqs/faq48-3e.htm> (April 23, 2000).

9. Arleigh Burke, "Foreword," in Winifred Quick Collins with Herbert M. Levine, *More Than a Uniform: A Navy Woman in a Navy Man's World* (Denton, Tex.: University of North Texas Press, 1997), p. ix.

10. "Negro Women to Be Accepted in Women's Reserve, U.S. Naval Reserve." Navy Department press release, 19 October 1944. *Naval Historical Center Page*. n.d. <http://www.history.navy.mil/faqs/faq57-6.htm> (April 21, 2000).

11. "What Is a Wave?"

12. "Women in the U.S. Military During Desert Shield/Desert Storm." From Appendix R, "Role of Women in the Theater of Operations," in *Conduct of the Persian Gulf War: Final Report to Congress*, vol. 2 (Washington, D.C.: Department of Defense, 1992). *Naval Historical Page*. n.d. <http://www.history.navy.mil/faqs/faq48-3f.htm> (April 23, 2000).

13. Paul Stillwell, ed., *The Golden Thirteen* (Annapolis, Md.: Naval Institute Press, 1993), p. xv.

14. Morris J. MacGregor, *Integration of the Armed Forces 1940–1965* (Washington, D.C.: Center for Military History, United States Army, 1985). *United States Army Page*. <http://www.army.mil/cmh-pg/books/integration/IAF-03.htm> (April 23, 2000).

15. Ibid.

16. Ibid.

17. Stillwell, p. xviii.

18. Ibid., p. 2.

19. MacGregor, chapter 3.

20. Ibid., p. 4.

21. Ibid., p. 3.

22. Ibid., p. 2.

23. Ibid., pp. 2, 3, 6–7, 11–12.

24. Stillwell, p. 275.

Chapter 7. The Future

1. Department of the Navy. "A Vision of Tomorrow's Challenges and Solutions," 1999 Posture Statement, Section VI. *United States Navy Page*. n.d. <http://www.chinfo.Navy.mil/navpalib/policy/fromsea/pos99/pos-sec6.html> (April 23, 2000).

2. "Forces and Manpower." Report of the Quadrennial Defense Review, Section 5. *United States Department of Defense Page*. n.d. <http://www.defenselink.mil/pubs/qdr/sec5.html> (April 23, 2000).

Glossary

aircraft carrier—The largest ship afloat, with over five thousand crewmen, used to launch and retrieve attack aircraft as its primary weapon.

auxiliary ships—Any of a large number of ships that support and replenish warships.

battleship—One of the largest and most heavily armed ship prior to the development of the aircraft carrier.

below—As a naval term, anywhere beneath the main deck of a ship.

Black Gang—The term used to designate enlisted men who worked in the engine and boiler rooms on steamships.

bow—The front end of a ship.

captain—The commander of a ship; also a rank in the navy equal to a colonel in the army.

convoy—A group of ships that travel together in formation for protection.

cruiser—A large warship, smaller than a battleship but larger than a destroyer.

CSS—Initials that stand for "Confederate States Ship," used to indicate a ship of the Confederate States of America (1861–1865).

depth charge—A container filled with explosives that is set to explode at a certain depth.

destroyer—A small warship used for protecting convoys and hunting for submarines.

dive-bomber—An aircraft that delivers its bombs after a long vertical dive from a high altitude—the major weapon in the U.S. victory at the Battle of Midway.

dreadnought—Originally the name of a British battleship, the HMS *Dreadnought*, the name was used to identify other large, heavily armored warships in the early twentieth century.

flight deck—The platform on aircraft carriers that is used for takeoff and landing.

fore and aft—Forward and backward.

gunner's mate—The officer in charge of the maintenance and care of a ship's weapons and ammunition.

HMS—Initials that stand for "His (Her) Majesty's Ship," used to indicate a ship of the British Navy.

main deck—The uppermost deck of a ship that extends from bow to stern (front to back).

man-of-war—A navy's combatant warship.

midshipman—An officer in training; the term comes from the practice of stationing such men in the middle of the ship to relay orders from the captain on the quarterdeck forward.

port—The left side of a ship when one is facing the bow (front).

quarterdeck—On sailing ships, the deck above the main deck that extends from the stern a quarter of the way to the bow.

rigging—On a sailing ship, the masts, sails, and ropes used to move the ship through the water.

sloop—A single-masted sailing ship with two sails.

starboard—The right side of a ship when one is facing the bow (front).

stern—The back end of a ship.

torpedo plane—An aircraft whose major weapon is a torpedo. It must expose itself to enemy fire in order to deliver its torpedo.

USS—Initials that stand for "United States Ship," used to indicate a ship of the United States of America.

Further Reading

Black, Wallace B. and Jean F. Blashfield. *Blockade-Runners and Ironclads: Naval Action in the Civil War*. Danbury, Conn.: Franklin Watts, 1997.

Burgan, Michael. *U.S. Navy Special Forces: SEAL Teams*. Danbury, Conn.: Franklin Watts, 1999.

Burgan, Michael. *U.S. Navy Special Forces: Special Boat Units*. Danbury, Conn.: Franklin Watts, 1999.

Green, Michael. *Aircraft Carriers*. Minnetonka, Minn.: Capstone Press, 1999.

Green, Michael. *The United States Navy*. Minnetonka, Minn.: Capstone Press, 1998.

Kraus, Theresa. *The Department of the Navy*. Broomall, Pa.: Chelsea House Publishers, 1990.

Pelta, Kathy. *The U.S. Navy*. Minneapolis: Lerner Publishing, 1990.

Internet Addresses

U.S. Navy Web site
(includes Naval Historical Web site)
<http://www.navy.mil>

Navy Jobs Web Site
<http://www.navyjobs.com>

U.S. Naval Academy Web site
<http://www.usna.edu>

Index

A

Adams, John Quincy, 19
African Americans, 8, 83, 89, 91, 93, 95, 96–100
aircraft carriers, 11–12, 27, 28, 29, 32, 37–38, 73, 75, 77, 95, 101, 102, 105
American Revolution, 13–14, 17, 91
Annapolis, Maryland, 50, 53, 95
apprentice system, 39, 41, 49
Atlantic Ocean, 13, 19, 27, 36, 37, 41, 95

B

Bancroft, George, 50
Barbary pirates, 17–18
Barclay, Robert Heriot, 8, 9, 10
basic training, 45, 47, 50
Battle of Lake Erie, 7–10, 11, 12, 42, 91
Battle of Manila, 22
Battle of Midway, 28–29, 32
battleships, 26, 27, 28, 33, 105, 107
Bonhomme Richard, 14, 15–16, 17
British Navy, 7, 14, 26, 34
Buchanan, Franklin, 50

C

cannons, 8, 9, 10, 15, 21, 23, 52, 69
Carter, Jimmy, 95
Chesapeake Bay, 23
Civil War, 19, 20, 22, 24, 54, 91
Clinton, William (Bill), 95
Confederacy, 20, 23
Congress, United States, 17, 26, 50, 87, 102, 104

Continental Congress, 14
cruisers, 12, 28, 32, 33, 37, 38, 75, 77, 95, 105
CSS *Alabama*, 19
CSS *David*, 23
CSS *Hunley*, 24
CSS *Sumter*, 19
CSS *Virginia*, 21, 23

D

Daniels, Josephus, 85, 87
D-Day, 33–34
Decatur, Stephen, Jr., 18
Department of Defense, 60, 62, 91
destroyers, 12, 26, 27, 28, 32, 33, 36, 38, 98, 107, 109, 113
Dewey, George, 22
dreadnoughts, 25–26, 28

E

Edison, Thomas A., 71
Ely, Eugene, 28, 105
engineering, 34, 56, 57, 69, 70, 73, 75, 80
English Channel, 33
enlistment, 44–45
    benefits, 76
    requirements for, 44

F

Farragut, David Glasgow, 49, 54
Fish, Stuyvesant, 84
frigates, 12, 23, 37, 38, 52, 54, 75, 77, 93
Fulton, Robert, 41, 113

G

Gay, George H., 29
Gravely, Samuel, 99

Great Britain, 7, 14, 17, 26, 27, 33, 114
Great Lakes, 7
Great White Fleet, 25, 26
Gulf of California, 22

H
Halsey, William F., Jr., 29
Harrison, William Henry, 10
Hiryu, 32
HMS *Argus*, 28, 105
HMS *Detroit*, 9, 10
HMS *General Hunter*, 9
HMS *Merriam*, 17
HMS *Queen Charlotte*, 9, 10
HMS *Serapis*, 15, 16, 17
HMS *Shannon*, 52
Hopper, Grace Murray, 48

I
ironclads, 20–21, 23, 24, 25, 109, 112

J
James River, 21
Jones, John Paul, 14–17

K
Knox, Frank, 96

L
Lake Erie, 7, 11, 12, 42, 91
Lawrence, James, 52
Leahy, W.D., 36

M
MacArthur, Douglas, 36
Madison, James, 7
Mallory, Stephen, 21
Mediterranean Sea, 17, 19, 38, 42
merchant ships, 13, 14, 15, 17, 27
Mexican War, 19, 42

midshipmen, 19, 49–50, 54, 84
Midway, 28, 32, 105
Miller, Doris, 95
minesweepers, 33, 77
missiles, 12, 37, 43, 80, 95, 105, 107, 109, 114
Monitor, 21, 23, 109, 112

N
Naval Academy, 22, 29, 34, 50, 53, 95
Naval Reserve, 45, 48, 53, 55, 59, 68, 85, 87, 88–89, 93
Nimitz, Chester William, 36
nuclear power, 25, 34, 37, 38, 42, 74, 75, 77, 80, 95, 105, 109
nurses, 53, 80, 87–88, 98

O
officer training, 49–50, 53, 55–57, 59, 70

P
Pacific Ocean, 27, 29, 36, 37
Pearl Harbor, Hawaii, 28, 29, 88, 95
Perry, Matthew Calbraith, 41, 42
Perry, Oliver Hazard, 7–10, 11, 41, 42, 91
Persian Gulf, 38, 91
Philippine Islands, 22, 88
Polk, James K., 50
Porter, David, 54
Preble, Edward, 17, 18

R
radar, 12, 73, 111
Reason, Joseph Paul, 95
recruiters, 43, 44, 45
restricted line officers, 77, 80
revolving turret, 21, 111–112

Rickover, Hyman George, 34
Roosevelt, Eleanor, 98
Roosevelt, Franklin D., 28,
    36, 88, 97, 98
Roosevelt, Theodore, 26

S
satellites, 12, 101
schooners, 8, 10
screw propeller, 112
Seabees, 97
SEALs, 77, 83
Semmes, Raphael, 19
sloops, 10, 23
Smalls, Robert, 93
sonar, 12, 73, 113
South China Sea, 38
staff corps officers, 77, 80
steam power, 34, 37, 41, 42,
    69–70, 112, 113–114
Stewart, Charles, 84
Straits of Gibraltar, 17
submarines, 12, 23–25, 26,
    27, 34, 36, 37, 38, 75,
    77, 80, 83, 99, 102, 105,
    109, 111, 113, 114

T
torpedoes, 24, 27, 29, 32, 93,
    107, 114

U
Union, 19, 20, 21, 22, 23, 24,
    93, 109
unrestricted line officers, 77,
    80
USS *Arizona*, 95
USS *Augusta*, 36
USS *Bainbridge*, 37, 95
USS *Chesapeake*, 52
USS *Clermont*, 113
USS *Congress*, 23

USS *Constitution*, 17, 18
USS *Cumberland*, 23
USS *Decatur*, 26, 36
USS *Demologos*, 113–114
USS *Enterprise*, 29, 37, 95
USS *Essex*, 54
USS *Fulton the First*, 114
USS *Fulton II*, 41, 42
USS *Holland*, 24
USS *Hopper*, 48
USS *Hornet*, 29
USS *Housatonic*, 24
USS *Kearsarge*, 19
USS *Lawrence*, 8–9, 10
USS *Long Beach*, 37
USS *Masin*, 99
USS *Maumee*, 36
USS *Merrimac*, 21
USS *Minnesota*, 23
USS *Nautilus*, 34
USS *Niagara*, 8, 9–10
USS *Philadelphia*, 18
USS *Trenton*, 71–72
USS *Triton*, 37
USS *Truxtun*, 95
USS *Winthrop*, 17
USS *Yorktown*, 29

W
War of 1812, 7, 49, 54, 87,
    91
WAVES, 88–91
Welles, Gideon, 21
women in the navy, 83–85,
    87–91
World War I, 24, 26–27, 36,
    73, 85, 87, 93
World War II, 27–29, 32–34,
    36, 48, 53, 73, 88–90,
    95–99, 111